Bread Around the World

by John Serrano

Who Eats Bread?

People all around the world eat bread. In fact, someone somewhere is eating bread as you read this book!

Some people eat bread for breakfast. People eat bread for lunch and dinner, too! When do you eat bread? What kinds of bread do you like?

What Size and Shape Is Bread?

Some breads are big, but some breads are little. Bread can be long and thin. This long, thin bread is from Europe.

▲ The baguette is from France.

Some breads are flat.
These flat breads are round.
People in many places
eat round, flat breads.

▼ This injera bread is from Africa.

India

Sweden

China

This round bread has a hole in the middle! Where did people make the first bagel? No one really knows!

▲ Bagels are shaped like doughnuts.

Breads can be twisted, like pretzels! People in Germany made the first pretzel.

Germany

Ukraine

Israel

▲ People can make many different shapes out of breads.

What Color Is Bread?

Most breads are a shade of brown. The flour bakers use to make many breads comes from grains. The grains are a shade of brown.

Some people use corn or rice to make flour. People can use nuts and beans, too!

▲ In Mexico, people make tacos from corn.

Most of the time, breads are the color of the flour people use to make the breads.

◀ Some people eat colored breads on holidays.

People can also use food coloring or vegetables to change the color of breads.

▲ This bread is green from mold!

What Do People Eat on Bread?

Some people like to eat butter on their bread. People in Italy dip their bread into olive oil.

◀ Olive oil and butter have similar tastes.

Some people eat fish on their bread. Do you eat fish on bread?

Many people eat cheese on their bread. Some people bake the cheese into the bread instead.

This cheese bread ▶ is from Colombia.

Do you like to eat chocolate? Some people eat chocolate on their bread! Many people eat their bread with nothing at all.

▲ Chocolate can make bread taste like a dessert.

People all over the world eat bread. Did you eat bread today?